50 TIPS
TO HELP YOU STAY
POSITIVE

50 TIPS TO HELP YOU STAY POSITIVE

Copyright © Summersdale Publishers Ltd, 2014

With research by Elanor Clarke

Vie Books is an imprint of Summersdale Publishers Ltd

Summersdale Publishers Ltd
46 West Street
Chichester
West Sussex
PO19 1RP
UK

www.summersdale.com

Printed and bound in the Czech Republic

ISBN: 978-1-84953-581-6

Substantial discounts on bulk quantities of Summersdale books are available to corporations, professional associations and other organisations. For details contact Nicky Douglas by telephone: +44 (0) 1243 756902, fax: +44 (0) 1243 786300 or email: nicky@summersdale.com.

50 TIPS
TO HELP YOU STAY
POSITIVE

Anna Barnes

Introduction

Remaining positive about yourself and your situation is key to your happiness. It can seem hard to remain on an even keel when life throws obstacles in your way: increasing work, home and even social commitments can seem to conspire to make us feel negative and unable to cope. This book is packed with easy-to-follow tips that can help you to put a positive spin on your situation and see the good in yourself. If, however, you find that low mood has started to affect your day-to-day life, it is recommended that you seek advice from your doctor.

SECTION ONE:

UNDERSTANDING POSITIVITY

Learning more about your positive and negative moods, and gaining a greater understanding of how they affect you, acts as a solid starting point for becoming more positive.

Keep a diary

Many people find keeping a diary cathartic as it provides a structured way to discuss and release emotions, as well as becoming a record of your recent history, which you can look back on in order to understand your feelings about and reactions to certain people, places and situations. Try focusing your diary entries on positive and negative feelings, ask yourself where and when you feel happiest, where you feel uncomfortable, and who affects your mood. Be honest with yourself and use this as a learning tool.

When choosing a diary, make sure it is one you will want to pick up and write in every day. Choose a design and layout that suit your tastes, and keep it somewhere you know you will see it or remember it, for example on a bookshelf or in your bedside drawer.

2

Talk to friends and family

When trying to better understand any subject, talking to other people can prove invaluable, and the topic of how to stay positive is no different. As this is a personal subject, ask your friends and family how they stay positive, or how they deal with negative feelings, and what their coping mechanisms are; you may be surprised by their answers. Getting a broad picture by asking people you trust to share their views and experiences can help you better understand how to achieve a positive mindset.

Be your own guide

Self-guided meditation can be an excellent starting point for understanding how you view events, both positive and negative, and how they affect you. Though many may view the act of meditation itself less than favourably, imagining extremely dedicated people sitting in the lotus position for hours on end, this is far from the truth. Meditation comes in many forms and, in this exercise, you are your own guide.

Sit in a comfortable position, or lie down if you prefer, and close your eyes. Think of an event in your life that has negative feelings attached to it. Try to relive this event in your mind, without judgement, while you focus on the emotions and thoughts that it stirs up. Throughout, be non-judgemental; simply allow thoughts and feelings to come up, and recognise them for what they are. Next, do the same for a positive, happier event. For both, try to immerse yourself in the sounds, smells and sights around you. This will help you to understand what has triggered positive and negative emotions. You may want to write down your findings in your diary, so that you can go back to them at any time.

Make a happy list

In order to focus on the positive, try making a list of all the good things in your life. This might seem difficult at first, but you can always ask friends and family for help. The list could be made up of personal or general points, for example 'I am healthy', or 'My family is supportive'. This is something you can pin in a prominent place to remind you of the good around you when negativity seems to be creeping in.

SECTION TWO:

EXERCISE FOR A MOOD BOOST

Exercise is a wonderful way to increase endorphins in the body, which help you stay in a positive frame of mind. It is easy to incorporate simple forms of activity into even the busiest schedule, and this will allow you a welcome break from the stresses and strains of day-to-day life.

5

Walk into positivity

Starting an exercise regime can seem daunting, especially if you are feeling negative. Joining a gym or going to a group class can seem like the last thing you would want to do. However, exercise can be as simple as going for a walk. Just a half-hour walk each day can significantly improve your health and emotional wellbeing. You can fit this in on the way to work, at lunchtime or whenever feels right for you. Try going for walks in daylight, in natural surroundings; the sunlight will warm your skin and should make you feel more positive as it produces mood-boosting vitamin D.

6

Practise yoga for body and mind

The ancient practice of yoga is not just about moving and stretching your body, but also about attaining balance, improved posture and peace of mind. Yoga is non-competitive and practised at your own pace, allowing you to take time to really understand what your body can do. It can help you to feel more positive because of the strengthening and toning effect it has on the body, and because of the calming effect it has on the mind. Most classes will finish with yogic sleep (Savasana), or guided meditation, which can leave you feeling refreshed, happier and more in touch with yourself. If you would rather not attend a class, you could try yoga at home with the help of books, DVDs or online demonstrations.

7

Dance yourself fit and happy

Dancing is, for many people, one of the most fun ways to get fit, and having fun alongside releasing the mood-boosting endorphins exercise provides, is a great positivity cocktail. This can be as simple as putting on your favourite music at home and dancing around your living room or bedroom, or you could try a class. Jive, jazz, ballroom and Latin classes are all great ways to get fit and meet new people, and fitness fusion classes such as Zumba are becoming ever-more popular. Choose a style that suits you and, above all, enjoy it.

SECTION THREE:

EAT WELL, FEEL WELL

As well as improving your general health, what you eat can have a huge impact on your emotional wellbeing. Try these dietary tips to help you feel better inside and out.

Stay balanced

The most important thing to bear in mind when trying to adopt a healthy-eating plan is to start with a balanced diet that incorporates all the major food groups. Once you have ensured that you are getting enough protein, fibre, fat, and plenty of vitamin-rich fruits and vegetables, you have a great starting point. If you are unsure of which foods are best for optimum health, a web search will provide you with comprehensive lists of foods rich in the nutrients you require, allowing you to plan healthier meals for your personal dietary requirements.

Learn to love whole grains

While it can be tempting to reach for a slice of cake or a biscuit when negativity strikes, it's important to remember that the refined flour and sugar combination in these foods can be detrimental to health and cause a wide variety of problems. These issues range from poor skin condition to serious illnesses such as diabetes, all of which can cause your mood to dip. Instead, try to incorporate more whole grains into your diet. This can be as simple as switching white bread for wholemeal, white rice for whole rice, or choosing a breakfast cereal that contains whole-grain rice. You could also try some of the many interesting grains available by getting creative with your cooking – why not try using bulgur wheat in a salad, or millet with a tagine – the combination options are endless.

Keep your GI low

A low-GI diet can have many health benefits – more steady energy levels, less bloating, no sugar cravings – all of which can help you to stay feeling positive. GI stands for glycaemic index; the ranking of carbohydrate-containing foods based on their overall effect on blood glucose levels. When we eat foods with a high GI, such as white bread, pastries and sweets, our blood sugar spikes and then rapidly drops, leaving us tired, irritable and hungry. Eating low-GI foods – such as beans, rye breads, and most fruit and veg – helps ensure your body is fuelled throughout the day and night, avoiding the spikes and dips in your blood sugar that can have a detrimental effect on your emotions, and therefore leaves you feeling more balanced.

Power up with protein

Protein is not just essential for building muscle, but is also important for managing hunger levels and improving mood. Proteins are made up of amino acids: the essential building blocks from which our body produces almost everything. In particular, the amino acids tryptophan and phenylalanine are great for the mood, as they are used in the production of the neurotransmitters serotonin, dopamine and adrenaline. These three hormones help you to feel happier and more motivated naturally, therefore giving your positivity a boost.

Feel good with fantastic fats

For many people, a healthy diet means a low-fat diet. Many 'healthy' products are marketed as low fat or fat free, and we are led to believe that eating fat makes you fat. This is, however, not entirely true. Fats are an important part of your diet. They are key in neurotransmitter production due to the amino acids they contain, and unsaturated fats are important for healthy skin and hair. As long as you get the balance right and are eating enough monounsaturated and polyunsaturated fats, such as those found in olive oil and seeds, and you are reducing the amount of saturated fat you consume, for example the fats in butter, cheese and red meat, you can begin to benefit physically, and the positive changes in your appearance and general health can give you a good mood boost.

Boost your B vitamins

B vitamins are particularly important for maintaining a balanced mood and therefore for feeling positive. Among their many functions, B vitamins are involved in the body's control of tryptophan, a building block for serotonin. Vitamin B6 is essential in the production of GABA (gamma-aminobutyric acid), which helps boost mood in a similar way to serotonin. A lack of these neurotransmitters can lead to low mood, which in turn can lead to serious psychological problems such as depression. The main vitamins to pay attention to are B1, B2, B3, B5, B6, B9 and B12, all of which can be found in a balanced diet. If you eat a lot of processed foods, or are a vegan, you may be lacking in certain B vitamins, in which case adding a B-vitamin supplement to your diet can have an excellent effect on your overall health and mood.

Be ACE

Low mood can make the body feel stressed, and high levels of stress hormones in your system can have a negative effect on your health, either by lowering your immune system, making you more prone to coughs, colds and other infections, or by over-stimulating it and provoking autoimmune illnesses and inflammation. A simple way to combat these symptoms is to eat plenty of foods rich in the antioxidant vitamins A, C and E. These antioxidants help normalise the body and reduce inflammation, while boosting immunity.

Vitamin A is found in the form of retinol in products such as fish livers and oils, and egg yolks. Too much retinol can be bad for the health though, so balance this with beta-carotene, mainly found in yellow and orange fruits and vegetables such as carrots, butternut squash and apricots. Vitamin C is found in good amounts in citrus fruits, broccoli, berries and tomatoes, and vitamin E is found in nuts, seeds, avocados, olive oil and wheatgerm. Adding some of these foods to your diet could make you feel healthier and happier, a great combination for positivity, as well as improving the look of your skin and hair, which can help with building a positive body image.

15

Moderate your alcohol intake

When feeling low or stressed after a difficult day, many people will reach for a drink to help them relax and unwind. Alcohol does have an instantly calming effect, but this is negated by its depressant qualities and the feeling of anxiety that can be left behind once the effect wears off. Alcohol can also disturb your sleep, contrary to the popular idea of a 'nightcap', and feeling tired and anxious can cause negative thinking. Try to cut down your drinking as much as possible and, if you do have a drink, opt for a small glass of Chianti, Merlot or Cabernet Sauvignon, as the plant chemicals – called procyanidins – that are abundant in these particular wines, are beneficial to health, especially cardiovascular health. These wines are also rich in melatonin, the sleep hormone, and a well-rested person is more likely to be a confident person.

SECTION FOUR:

REMOVE STRESS,
BUILD POSITIVITY

Stress is one of the biggest causes of illness and unhappiness in modern society. It can take many forms, and affects everyone in different ways, so try these tips to reduce your stress levels and feel all the more positive.

16

Understand your stressors

As individuals, we all have different needs in all aspects of our lives, therefore we have different stress factors in our lives. While there are several broad issues that often cause stress in the majority of people, we tend to know ourselves best, and can work out which things affect us the most; these are known as 'triggers' or 'stressors'. Identifying your triggers and making small, manageable changes are important steps in de-stressing. For example, it may be that driving to work makes you stressed, or going for big nights out. In these instances, why not try getting the bus to work, or arranging smaller social gatherings with your friends?

17

De-stress your home

Although you may not realise it, your home can be a very stressful place. Whether you have too much clutter around you, too many demands on your time and resources, or perhaps you don't feel comfortable in your home, these are some of the ways in which the home environment can become a stressor. Try reducing stress by using simple cleaning and decluttering methods. Make sure you only keep things you really need – unwanted clutter can be sold via websites such as

Gumtree or eBay, or given to charity shops. When cleaning, start in one room and clean it from the back to the front. Divide the house room by room and do one each day, if that helps. These steps will make your home a more comfortable environment and help you feel positive about where you live, and your ability to stay on top of chores.

Make your workplace calm

The workplace is, for many of us, the most stressful environment we can find ourselves in. Workplace stress is often a source of concern for people, and can leave us feeling very negative. To make your workplace feel calmer, try adding some plants to your desk area, as they not only brighten up the place and give you some of the calming benefits of nature but help oxygenate the environment. It is equally important to make sure you take regular breaks from your work to avoid feeling overburdened, even if you just go to make a drink. Finally, avoid letting other people's stress rub off on you. Stress can be 'caught', so if a colleague is complaining and being overly negative, either move the conversation away from the subject or, if you can't, excuse yourself and spend some time away from them.

Make a budget and stick to it

Financial worries are one of today's biggest stressors, with more and more people in increasing debt and/or out of work. Taking control of your finances is a great way to make you feel more positive as it helps to reduce the stress that can bring your mood down, and it shows that you can take on a difficult situation and improve it.

Some simple ways to cut back on non-essential spending are: cancel any direct debits for services you do not want or need. For example, do you have subscriptions for apps or services you hardly use? Next, look at debt: make sure you are paying off the debts with the highest interest rates first, so you save money on interest. Getting expert advice on your debts and how to manage them is a good idea, especially if you are not sure where to start. The free Money Advice Service (www.moneyadviceservice.org.uk) can help, so this needn't be a further expense.

Finally, make sure you spend your money on the things that are most important to you. For example, do you enjoy eating out with your partner or with friends? If so, make sure you put some money aside for it. Are the brands you use important to you? If not, you could cut costs by choosing shops' own-brand products.

20

Avoid 'sticky' situations

It is likely that when you look at your triggers, certain situations or even people come up as major stressors. One of the best ways to remove stress, in the short term at least, is to avoid these people and situations wherever possible. Politely decline social situations that make you feel stressed; when you are feeling more positive, you could always confront those stressors and hopefully remove or reverse the effect they have on you for good.

SECTION FIVE:

SLEEP WELL, FEEL MORE POSITIVE

Making sure you get a good night's sleep is essential to staying positive. Sleep is what keeps us feeling refreshed and focused, so try these tips for better-quality sleep and therefore improved mood.

Learn how much sleep you need

We are told that the average adult needs eight hours' sleep each night, but we are not all average. Knowing what is normal for you can help you to be sure that you are not oversleeping or getting too little sleep, either of which can be a source of concern. It may help to keep a sleep diary, or to use an app that tells you the optimum time to wake up, taking into consideration your chosen bedtime. Many apps give several options based on the number of full sleep cycles you require. Changing our perceptions of the amount we need to sleep can help us to feel more secure, and therefore help us sleep more easily, with a better quality of sleep, which leaves us more rested and ready to take on new challenges with a positive outlook.

Love your bedroom

Poor-quality sleep can have as much of an effect on your mood as lack of sleep. To help ensure that you feel great and ready to start the day each morning, make your bedroom into your personal sanctuary. Experts advise that bedrooms should be for sleep and sex only, so remove all distractions; do away with the computers and televisions, and even, if you can, your mobile phone. If you would usually use your mobile as an alarm, try investing in an alarm clock to help you keep technology out of the bedroom. Keep paperwork out of the bedroom by opening your post elsewhere, and save important discussions for other rooms. Finally, make sure your space is tidy and inviting; soon you will be sleeping soundly and feeling more positive from the moment you wake up.

23

Choose bed linen that makes you feel good

Having bedding that suits you and helps you to feel better about yourself and your surroundings can give you a great positivity boost; as well as the benefit to your quality of sleep, attractive linen helps make your bedroom a place you are proud of, and that you feel comfortable and relaxed in.

Choosing the right bed linen means choosing something that will make you feel cosy and ready to sleep in the evening, and fresh and ready to go in the morning. For some people, cool cotton sheets and duvet covers work best; others find silk gentler against their skin. For many people, synthetic fabrics make them sweat too much in the night, which can cause night-time waking, leaving you unrefreshed and even jittery. Invest in a couple of sets of good linen, rather than multiple cheap and cheerful sets of polyester sheets, to help you feel more positive about your bedroom.

Darkness is best

Like sound, light can disturb your sleep and cause early waking, which then leads to poor-quality rest and irritability, leaving you feeling negative and ill-prepared for the day ahead. While darkness causes your brain to produce melatonin, the hormone that makes you feel sleepy, light helps it produce serotonin, too much of which will make you feel more awake.

To help keep your bedroom as dark as possible, make sure any electrical items such as stereos are turned off, not on standby, as the lights from their displays may keep you awake. Your mobile phone, if you must use it as an alarm, should be in bedside mode so that it does not emit light. You should also choose thick, dark curtains or blinds, to ensure outside light does not intrude and wake you. If light is a particular nuisance for you, try using blackout curtains or blinds in your bedroom, or using an eye mask while you sleep.

Have a silent, restful night

Noise can be a big cause of sleep disturbance. This can be anything from a ticking clock, to sirens outside, to a snoring partner. It is likely that you will already know which noises usually wake you up or disturb your sleep. In an ideal world, you would remove these sounds completely, but this is not always possible. There are many things you can easily do, however, like removing the battery from a ticking clock at night and using a digital clock as an alarm, or fixing the dripping tap that keeps you awake. This can help the quality of your sleep improve and, with it, help you feel more equipped for the challenges of your day.

26

Cleanliness for positivity

We all feel good when we're fresh from the bath or shower, and keeping that fresh feeling in the bedroom helps to improve sleep and keep us positive. Bed linen that is freshly washed will feel cool and comforting against the skin. It is important to wash your sheets once a week, or more often if you have been unwell or if the weather is particularly hot. If you have the chance to, try air-drying your sheets on a line for added freshness.

Less screen time, more sleep

Most of us spend ever-increasing amounts of time in front of screens each day – computers, tablets, televisions and smartphones are core parts of most people's lives. These sorts of backlit screens, however, are detrimental to our sleep cycles. It may seem like watching a film or reading an article on your tablet is a good way to unwind before bed, but these activities make the brain more alert, and therefore make it harder to switch off at night. Bright screens halt the production of the sleep hormone, melatonin, in a similar way to daylight. Instead, try reading a book in gentle light, or listening to some calming music, to help you drift off.

Relax, step by step

Both meditation and yoga teach us that progressive relaxation is an excellent way to aid sleep. It is often the case that when low mood strikes and we feel negative, we lie awake at night unable to relax. This simple exercise will help you to relax your body and ease your mind in preparation for a good night's sleep.

Concentrating on each body part at a time, start at your feet and work your way up your body. For each body part, clench it as tightly as you can before letting it go and feel the physical relaxation that comes with this release. Some people find it helpful to use a verbal aid, for example by saying or thinking 'I am relaxing my feet, my feet are now completely relaxed', and repeating for each body part.

SECTION SIX:

BE KIND TO YOURSELF

Being good to yourself is an easy and enjoyable way to stay positive. Giving yourself treats and taking care of yourself on the outside can give you a boost inside.

Invest in some 'me time'

It is all too easy to believe that all your time should be spent doing 'useful' things, or being there for other people. This is, however, not true, and trying to keep going all the time for the sake of others, without giving yourself the space to just enjoy your own company, will leave you feeling drained and tired, allowing negativity to creep in.

For a positivity boost, try taking the night off. Indulge in your favourite foods, watch a film or series that you love, pick up a book you've been meaning to read and, most importantly, switch off from the rest of the world. Perhaps you want to pamper yourself too, giving your feet a soak or indulging in an extra-long bath. You will likely feel all the more positive for giving your batteries a chance to recharge.

30

Look after your skin

Healthy-looking skin is the basis for feeling good about your looks. Seeing someone healthy when you look at yourself in the mirror can give you a boost and make you feel more positive. Put simply, when you look good, it is more likely you will feel good. To keep your skin in the best shape, make sure you cleanse and moisturise regularly. You don't need to buy expensive products, as cheaper brands usually contain the same key ingredients. Just ensure that the product is designed for your skin type, for example, dry, oily, combination or normal.

Another important factor to remember is sunscreen. While it is easy to remember the suncream on a hot day, the truth is that it should be worn most of the time. The easiest way to protect your skin is to use a daytime moisturiser with added SPF. Getting a little time in the sun, however, is good for you. Up to 15 minutes without suncream will not only feel great on your skin, but will also help to boost your vitamin D and serotonin levels, which in turn improves mood.

Have a good hair day

Looking after your hair is an excellent way to improve the way you feel about your body, in the same way that keeping your skin looking great will make you feel good about yourself. Make sure you wash and condition as often as you need to, with products designed for your hair type: for example, dry, oily, coloured or curly. If you feel in need of a bigger boost, why not invest in a hair masque to pamper yourself with, or try out a new haircut or colour to show the new, more positive you. Be daring and show your personal style, and feel your positive energy building.

32

Nail it

Treating yourself to either a manicure or pedicure can be a fun way to help you stay positive about your physical self. This doesn't have to entail long, painted nails, unless you want it to. It also doesn't need to be expensive, with many daily deals websites offering treatments, and nail bars often running special deals for new clients. Simple manicure and pedicure treatments can include massage, trimming and filing of nails, buffing and cleaning, all of which can be done to even the shortest of nails, helping you stay well-groomed and feeling good.

Dress the way *you* want to

Just like your new bed linen, making sure that your wardrobe reflects your personality and style can help boost your positivity. Start by decluttering your current wardrobe and throwing out anything too old, especially if it does not fit or is unflattering. These clothes don't have to go to waste; they can, just like household clutter, be sold online through websites such as eBay or Gumtree, or taken to a local charity shop.

Once you are left with your basics and favourites, replenish with clothes that make you feel good. The way you dress affects the way you feel, from the colours you choose to how an item fits. The old adage says, 'Dress for the job you want, not the one you have.' Choose well-fitting clothes that reflect your personality and where you want to be in your life. Make sure that when you look in the mirror, what you are wearing makes you think 'Yes, I look good today', rather than 'What am I wearing' or 'It will have to do'. Feeling good in your clothes will make you feel more comfortable in yourself, and boost your self-image both in the workplace and socially.

34

Laugh more

Though it may seem too simple, the act of laughing makes people feel more positive. When you laugh out loud, natural endorphins are released, which give you feelings of happiness. Laughter is also good for you, helping to keep your blood pressure healthy and helping you to sleep more soundly. Try watching your favourite comedy, or getting together for a good laugh with friends or family, for a positivity lift.

Learn something new

Learning is one of the best gifts you can give yourself, and learning something new can help with positivity in several ways. Firstly, new knowledge or skills will give your confidence a lift, and make you feel more positive about your abilities. Secondly, if you attend a class, meeting people there is a great way to enhance your social life. Finally, learning something new gives you the opportunity to talk to your loved ones about your new experiences.

What you choose to learn can be anything from a new language to drawing, and anything in between. Choose something which you think will enrich your life and, above all, enjoy it.

SECTION SEVEN:

DO MORE FOR OTHERS

Doing more for others, as long as you are leaving time for yourself, can help build positivity. Not only are you likely to enjoy the activities suggested in these tips, but you will be making somebody else feel good too – a positive cocktail.

36

Walk a dog

Although you may not have a dog of your own, it is likely you have a friend or family member who owns one. Offering to walk a friend's pet frees up time for them to do more for themselves, while giving you the opportunity to get out into nature and share that with an animal companion. Dog walking is a positive experience for both you and the pet; not only does it offer the chance for some green exercise for both you and the dog, but it is well known that spending time with animals gives a boost to the mood.

37

Organise a movie night with friends

Having a get-together with friends and family is good for everyone involved. Be the host and arrange for a group of people to come to your place for a movie night. Perhaps each person could pick their favourite film, or there could be a themed double or triple bill. Take the time to catch up with everyone and see how they are doing, let yourself be the gracious host and be there for your friends, whether they need to talk, need a shoulder to cry on or just require some good company.

38

Write a letter

Most of us have relatives or friends who live at the other end of the country, or have even emigrated. Give yourself and them a boost by sitting down to write a letter by hand, letting them know what you've been up to and asking them plenty of questions. Use this as an opportunity to catch up in a way you wouldn't be able to over the phone or via Facebook, by being honest and open, and perhaps sending a little memento such as a photograph along with your note. You will most likely get a hand-written reply, too, which will add to the sense of achievement and satisfaction.

39

Volunteer locally

Charities and voluntary organisations are always in need of help. Why not use some of your spare time to help out at a local animal rescue centre or charity shop, or even give out leaflets? You can get in touch with charities easily through their websites and they will let you know where they need help most. Using your time constructively and helping a charitable cause is a great way to make you feel more positive about yourself, and about the way you use your free time.

SECTION EIGHT:

A POSITIVE MINDSET

The human brain is a very powerful thing. It can heal us and it can hinder us. These tips show you how to recognise when negative thoughts are causing problems and how to use the power of your mind to feel more positive.

Know a thought

Each of us will have as many as 50,000 thoughts every day. These can be simple things, such as, 'What should I watch tonight', or they can be powerful, such as 'I'm not a good enough partner'. Part of the concept of mindfulness, a way of recognising and understanding your thoughts and actions which is based on Buddhist teachings, is understanding that thoughts are simply thoughts. They have no substance and do not need to control the way you feel and behave. Repeating the same negative thought pattern for many years may have had a detrimental effect on your emotional state, leaving you feeling negative and drained, but once you can recognise this negativity as simply a thought, you can begin to challenge it and rebuild your self-concept.

Try positivity mantras

A mantra is a positive phrase that you repeat to yourself. Mantras can be thought or said out loud. Many people believe that actually saying your mantra makes it more effective, as vocalising something gives it more substance. You can also write your chosen mantra down and put it somewhere you are likely to see it, such as the kitchen or bathroom. Choose your mantra based on what is important to you, not what you feel others will accept; it could be anything, from 'I will pass my exam' to 'I am a good, honest person'. Regularly repeating your chosen mantra will help you reaffirm your faith in yourself and your abilities.

42

Be happy with you

Perfectionism can be destructive; continually striving for a perceived version of perfection can stop you from being happy with who you already are and from seeing all the positive things you already achieve. One of the most common perfectionist tendencies is to compare yourself with others. This may take the form of direct comparison, such as 'Viresh is more successful at work than I am' or of general comparison along the lines of 'I wish I could be more like Lily'. Either way, in seeing others as somehow better than you, you are moving your focus away from your positives. In trying to be like other people, you stop yourself from being the best version of you. Try instead to think about what areas of your life you would like to improve, and work on those areas without comparing with others, while recognising your strong points.

43

Be positively assertive

It can sometimes seem like the easier option to bow to the wishes of others and say 'yes' to everything, even if you are really not happy with a situation; this can lead to negativity towards both yourself for giving in, and to others for 'making' you do things you don't want to. Far from being easier on yourself, you are essentially telling yourself that the wishes of others are more important than your own. Being assertive doesn't have to mean being aggressive. The main thing is that you realise that your own needs are as important as everybody else's.

Try out these simple scenarios: your boss asks you to take on a new project when you are already overworked and you know that you will not be able to finish it to the necessary standard. Instead of taking it on because you think it is the correct thing to do, explain the situation to your boss, so that a solution can be found. Your friend asks you to go out, saying you will enjoy it. You know that what you really want to do today is to stay at home and read a book. Instead of going out to please your friend, talk to them and let them know that you are not in the mood, and that you will see them soon for another event. The likelihood is that they will appreciate your honesty.

44

Speak with power

It is common that, if we feel negative, it comes across in the way we speak. People may observe that our voice is high pitched, shaky or too quiet. Public speaking, in particular, can be very difficult, and worry may cause your voice to become higher pitched as your vocal cords tighten. You may also end up speaking in a way that lacks authority. This can cause a vicious circle of self-doubt, as you may not feel listened to or respected. To improve this situation, try speaking with power; let your tone be deeper, and keep your words slow and steady. Say what you want to say, like you mean it, and see the difference it can make. If you try this in front of a mirror it can be even more helpful, as you get used to seeing yourself talk, and act as your own audience. Seeing yourself progress to speaking calmly and with power can help you to overcome nerves if you have to speak publicly.

SECTION NINE:

TRY THERAPIES

Complementary therapies can provide the additional support you need to stay positive. They are widely available and varied enough that there is something to suit everybody.

45

Reflexology for calm

Reflexology is similar to the ancient art of acupressure, using stimulation of certain points to help the flow of energy through the body. These points are found on the feet, hands and face, but practitioners will usually use the feet as they are more sensitive and are believed to have pressure points that relate to every part of the body. Stimulating these points is supposed to release energy blockages in the related body part, therefore facilitating the free flow of energy through that body part, and helping to reduce illness. The relaxation alone can help reduce stress and make you feel more balanced and positive. For practicality, if you decide to try this on yourself, it may be easier to use your hands. Although reflexology can be self-practised, it is more beneficial to visit a trained reflexologist for treatment. Look up your local natural health centre for more information.

Improve your energy with Reiki

Reiki is an energy practice that works in a similar way to massage or acupressure. In Reiki, however, the therapist will usually not make direct contact with you, rather, they will hold their hands a short distance from your body in certain areas in order to massage your energy field. Reiki practitioners believe that we not only have energy flowing through our bodies, but that this energy is palpable in a field outside of ourselves, and that, using this field, they can improve mood disturbances and heal illness. Why not seek out a Reiki therapist at your local natural health centre, or online.

Alexander Technique for positivity

The Alexander Technique is a method developed by Frederick Matthias Alexander, an actor who realised his tense muscles were getting in the way of him performing at his best, due to a stress reaction causing the body to adopt unnatural posture. The technique is a series of simple posture exercises, which help you to relearn your natural, comfortable posture, and help you to look and feel your best, which is a great positivity boost. Going to see an Alexander Technique specialist will help you stand straight and tall, looking and feeling ready to take on whatever life throws at you.

Indulge in aromatherapy

Aromatherapy uses essential oils from plants to help calm or stimulate the mind and body. To keep your mood positive, try using stimulating oils such as geranium, rosemary or peppermint, or uplifting scents such as rose, bergamot or neroli. These can be used traditionally for massage, steam inhalation or as bath oils, but they can also be used around your home or workplace to help bring your mood up throughout the day. Try sprinkling some drops on a pomander to put in a drawer with your clothes, or using your favourite oil on some unscented potpourri. You can also get roll-on essential oils, which you use in a similar way to perfumes, putting them on your wrist where the warmth will disperse the uplifting scent around you all day.

49

Use supplements

Mood changes are often due to imbalances in our body and, as an extra way to keep your mood positive, supplements can be very helpful. If you talk to someone at your local health food shop or natural pharmacy, they will be able to give you advice on what is best for you, personally. The herbal supplements that are most likely to help you stay positive are those that help boost the mood and reduce stress, for example 5-HTP (5-hydroxytryptophan), which helps to boost natural serotonin levels; or passiflora (passion flower), which helps with calm and sleep. These are widely available, and 5-HTP can be taken as a tablet, whereas passiflora can come in tablet or tincture form, or be drunk as an infusion.

50

And finally… see your doctor

Although the tips in this book can help you stay positive, if you feel that negativity has taken over your life in an unhealthy way, and is having a detrimental effect on your health, the best advice is to consult with your GP. Negativity and low mood can be signs of more serious underlying conditions and your doctor may suggest a talking therapy such as CBT, or the use of medication, to get you back to where you want to be.

Notes

....
....
....
....
....
....
....
....
....
....
....
....
....
....
....

If you're interested in finding out more about our books,
find us on Facebook at **Summersdale Publishers**
and follow us on Twitter at **@Summersdale**.

www.summersdale.com